Table of Contents

About Dynamic Path

Dynamic Path has a simple mission statement: To help you pass your test and get ahead by providing high-quality study questions. Whether you're preparing for a real estate agent licensure or an AP exam, we want to help you succeed.

We believe in our content, and we offer 50 free practice questions for each of our exams on our site. You can take a sample test or study session with us online, and get the results emailed to you.

All exam modules are written and edited by experts in their field, and each practice question is accompanied by a detailed explanation.

There are several ways to learn with Dynamic Path. You can browse exams and learn on the site or through our mobile apps, available for iOS, Mac, Android, Kindle, and Windows.

Dynamic Path is a product of Upward Mobility, a 100% woman- and minority-owned company (SOWMBA-certified) based in Boston, MA. It was formed to create free and low-cost high-quality education and test preparation material that is witty, engaging, and adds value to the learning process. You can learn more about our social mission and values here, or read a message from one of our co-founders here. You can also learn more about our staff here.

If you have any questions, suggestions, or technical problems, feel free to email us at support@dynamicpath.com.

Happy studying!

Questions

Allergens & Intolerances

1. Food Allergy Research and Education (FARE) estimates how many Americans suffer from food allergies?

    A. 1 million Americans
    B. 10 million Americans
    C. 15 million Americans
    D. 30 million Americans

2. True or False. The number of people suffering from food allergies is decreasing over time.

    A. True
    B. False

3. What is a food allergy?

    A. When the immune system responds to unhealthy food.
    B. A minor condition that results in some discomfort;
    C. When the immune system mistakenly labels a harmless protein as toxic.
    D. When the immune system labels harmful proteins as toxic.

4. True or False. While food allergies are inconvenient, they are not life-threatening.

    A. True
    B. False

5. True or False. Food allergies can be serious enough to send a person to the emergency room.

    A. True
    B. False

6. How many emergency room visits are food allergy related per year?

    A. 200
    B. 5,000
    C. 200,000
    D. 500,000

7. Which of the following are examples of "Big 8" food allergies:

    A. Edamame
    B. Chicken tenders
    C. Spinach
    D. Strawberries

8. **How many different foods can cause allergic reactions?**

> A. The Big 8 foods only.
> B. More than 160 different foods.
> C. Researchers still do not know.
> D. 30.

9. **Which of the following are examples of "Big 8" allergens?**

> A. Milk, honey, and eggs.
> B. Walnuts, sea bass, and strawberries.
> C. Shrimp, whole-wheat bread, and milk.
> D. Peanuts, soybeans, and honey.

10. **Which population experiences the highest occurrences of food allergies?**

> A. The elderly
> B. Adults 14-30
> C. Men
> D. Children

11. **Jillian has a severe allergy to peanuts, if she inadvertently ingests peanuts what should she do?**

> A. Lie down and sleep it off.
> B. Call 911.
> C. Call a friend to talk about she should do.
> D. Wait and see what happens.

12. **The "Big 8" are important because:**

> A. They represent the only known food allergies
> B. They include milk, soy beans and peanuts
> C. They are responsible for 50% of all allergic reactions
> D. They are responsible for 90% of all allergic reactions

13. **Sometimes adverse reactions to foods, including allergies and intolerances, are covered by what umbrella term?**

> A. Food preferences
> B. Genetic tolerance
> C. Food sensitivities
> D. Celiac disease

14. **Which is an example of a food intolerance?**

> A. Dairy allergy.
> B. Celiac disease.
> C. Both **A** and **B**.
> D. None of the above.

15. **Which of the following is an example of a food allergy?**

> A. Lactose intolerance
> B. Dislike for dairy
> C. Digestive upset from dairy
> D. Immune reaction to dairy

16. **When George eats ice cream, his body perceives the protein in dairy as an invader and his immune system acts to destroy it. George's reaction to ice cream can best be described as:**

    A. Lactose intolerance.
    B. Dairy allergy.
    C. Gluten intolerance.
    D. Gluten allergy.

17. **When Ellie eats soy products, she experiences digestive upset and discomfort. Ellie's reaction to soy can best be described as:**

    A. Celiac Disease.
    B. Soy allergy.
    C. Soy intolerance.
    D. Nutrient deficiency.

18. **Gluten is found in which of the following?**

    A. Wheat
    B. Rye
    C. Barley
    D. All of the above

19. **Which of the following can be life threatening?**

    A. Peanut allergy
    B. Soy intolerance
    C. Lactose intolerance
    D. Hives

20. **Which of the following would trigger symptoms in a person with Celiac Disease?**

    A. Eating wheat
    B. Drinking milk
    C. Eating soy
    D. All of the above

21. **Celiac Disease is an example of a(n):**

    A. Intolerance.
    B. Soy allergy.
    C. Autoimmune disease.
    D. Personal preference.

22. **True or False. There is a cure for Celiac Disease.**

    A. True
    B. False

23. **True or False. The only cure for a food allergy is Epinephrine.**

    A. True
    B. False

24. **How soon after ingesting a food can symptoms of an allergic reaction occur?**

    A. Immediately.
    B. Within a week.
    C. Within hours.
    D. Answers A and C.

25. **Which of the following is a symptom of an allergic reaction?**

    A. Hives
    B. Dizziness
    C. Fatigue
    D. All of the above

26. **Which of the following is NOT a symptom of an allergic reaction?**

    A. Itchy rashes
    B. Abdominal pain
    C. Migraine
    D. Swelling

27. **When a guest places a special order due to an allergy, they are trusting you with:**

    A. Their health.
    B. Their safety.
    C. Answers A and B.
    D. None of the above.

28. **Laura has an allergy to shellfish and tree nuts. If she experiences swelling of the face, hives, and trouble breathing, what might she have ingested?**

    A. Ice cream
    B. Peanuts
    C. Lobster
    D. Salmon

29. **Trevor is highly allergic to peanuts. If he ingested peanuts by mistake what allergic reaction symptom might he experience?**

    A. Vertigo
    B. Fever
    C. Swelling
    D. Tremor

30. **There are several common symptoms of an allergic reaction including hives, nausea, and:**

    A. Diarrhea.
    B. Wheezing.
    C. Answers A and B.
    D. None of the above.

31. Symptoms like abdominal pain and hives are common during an allergic reaction. There can also be swelling of the:

    A. Feet.
    B. Hands.
    C. Face.
    D. All of the above.

32. Monica is experiencing nausea, diarrhea, and abdominal pain after eating dairy products. She is most likely experiencing:

    A. Lactose intolerance.
    B. Anaphylaxis.
    C. Seasonal pollen allergies.
    D. Anxiety.

Food Handling

1. When there is a designated person to assist a guest with a food allergy, what is that person's job?

    A. To take the guest's order.
    B. To add garnishes before serving the order.
    C. To take the guest's order, communicate it to the chef, and take the correct plate to the right guest without any cross-contact.
    D. To take the guest's order, cook the order; add appropriate garnishes, sides, and sauces; and take the correct plate to the right guest without any cross-contact.

2. What information should a server include on the ticket of a guest with a food allergy?

    A. The time the order was made
    B. The guest's name
    C. The number of people in the party
    D. The date

3. Who does the server need to tell about an allergen special order?

    A. The entire staff
    B. The manager
    C. The hosts
    D. The chef

4. Which of the following is a system for identifying allergen special orders?

    A. A color-coded plate system
    B. Assigning letters randomly
    C. Using any color plate
    D. Not adding garnishes

5. Who on the staff needs to understand the policy about handling allergen special orders?

    A. Servers only
    B. Everyone
    C. Front of the house staff
    D. Back of the house staff

6. True or False: Confirming an allergen special order meal at pickup is mandatory.

    A. True
    B. False

7. What should the person delivering the allergen special order do at pickup?

    A. Chat with the chef about the order.
    B. Add garnishes and sauces.
    C. Confirm that it is the allergen special order.
    D. Find the original server to deliver the allergen special order.

8. **Before serving an allergen special order to the guest, what can be done to prevent cross-contact?**

    A. Allowing the food to cool first.
    B. Adding extra garnishes.
    C. Not adding garnishes.
    D. Adding sides to the dish.

9. **Who is the best person to deliver a meal to a guest with food allergies?**

    A. The manager
    B. The designated person.
    C. The chef.
    D. The server.

10. **True or False: It is okay to stack plates beside or on top of an allergen special order when delivering them to the guest's table.**

    A. True
    B. False

11. **Which of the following happens first?**

    A. The kitchen prepares the allergen special order and plates it on a red allergen plate.
    B. The server asks the table whether they enjoyed their meal.
    C. The designated person adds garnishes and sauces.
    D. The manager serves the order to the guest.

12. **If cross-contact occurs and is caught by staff before the dish goes to the guest, what should be done about it?**

    A. The manager should be contacted immediately.
    B. The chef should be contacted immediately.
    C. Depending on the severity of the contact, the food may be okay to serve to the guest.
    D. The food should be discarded and remade.

13. **In the case of an allergic reaction emergency, employees should:**

    A. Wait for someone to do something.
    B. Call 911.
    C. Get out of the way by going home.
    D. Shout loudly over the commotion.

14. **Cross-contact refers to when two foods come into contact so that their _____ mix.**

    A. Viruses
    B. Bacteria
    C. Proteins
    D. Carbohydrates

15. **True or False. For cross-contact to occur, large amounts of two different foods must come together and mix.**

    A. True
    B. False

16. **Which is an example of cross-contract?**

    A. Putting cheese on a sandwich.
    B. Using dirty utensils.
    C. Not washing hands.
    D. All of the above.

17. **True or False. Cross-contact and cross-contamination mean the same thing.**

    A. True
    B. False

18. **Cross-contamination occurs when what is transferred between two foods?**

    A. Protein
    B. Disease-causing organisms
    C. Carbohydrates
    D. Shellfish

19. **Which of the following can cause foodborne illness?**

    A. Food allergy
    B. Food intolerance
    C. Cross-contamination
    D. Cross-contact

20. **Which is the correct example of a proper cleaning procedure?**

    A. Cleaner, rinse, and sanitizer buckets with disposable paper towels.
    B. Cleaner, rinse, and sanitizer spray bottles with disposable paper towels.
    C. Cleaner spray bottle with disposable paper towels.
    D. Cleaner buckets with disposable paper towels.

21. **Meredith handles cheese while making a cheese-free sandwich for a guest with a dairy allergy. This is an example of:**

    A. Cross-contact.
    B. Contamination.
    C. Cross-Contamination.
    D. Foodborne illness.

22. **Food proteins can be found on:**

    A. Surfaces.
    B. Clothing.
    C. Hands.
    D. All of the above.

23. **True or False. Cooking foods to the right temperature can prevent foodborne illness.**

   A. True
   B. False

24. **Cross-contact involves the transfer of _______, while cross-contamination involves the transfer of _________**

   A. Proteins, disease-causing organisms
   B. Disease-causing organisms, protein
   C. Disease-causing organisms, bacteria
   D. Bacteria, viruses

25. **Which of the following examples would help prevent cross-contact?**

   A. Changing aprons and using hand sanitizer.
   B. Using hand sanitizer and using clean utensils.
   C. Using clean utensils and washing hands.
   D. None of the above.

Food Labels

1. Which is NOT an example of "May Contain" statements?

    A. "This product does not contain..."
    B. "May contain..."
    C. "Processed in a facility that also processes..."
    D. "Contains..."

2. What ingredients are food labels legally required to list?

    A. The unhealthy ones
    B. The Big 8 allergens
    C. Ingredients high in sodium
    D. Ingredients high in fat

3. If peanuts are listed in the ingredients list, is a manufacturer required to list it with the ingredients in a "Contains" list?

    A. No
    B. Yes
    C. Sometimes
    D. None of the above

4. Who regularly uses food label reading skills?

    A. Chefs
    B. Cooks
    C. Receiving staff
    D. All of the above

5. Casein and cream are derived from what Big 8 food?

    A. Milk
    B. Shellfish
    C. Fish
    D. Eggs

6. Miso and edamame are other names for what Big 8 food?

    A. Shellfish
    B. Soy
    C. Tree nuts
    D. Milk

7. Filbert and almonds may be listed on a food label and fall into what Big 8 category?

    A. Tree nuts
    B. Wheat
    C. Peanuts
    D. Soy

8. **How must allergens be legally listed on food packages?**

    A. In the title of the food.
    B. On the food's website.
    C. On the menu.
    D. In the "Contains" list.

9. **Which of the following would be the best to keep guests safe?**

    A. Keeping all foods containing allergens in an "allergen only" room.
    B. Keeping all allergens out of the kitchen from the start.
    C. Hoping cross-contact does not occur.
    D. Not serving any foods containing allergens.

10. **How can your operation keep allergens out of the kitchen?**

    A. Ordering from specialty suppliers that cater to allergen special orders.
    B. Labeling all packaged products.
    C. Hoping allergens do not come in contact with allergen special orders.
    D. There is nothing you can do to keep allergens out of the kitchen.

Kitchen and Prep

1. True or False. A great way to store allergen special order foods is in a designated area for allergen-free foods.

    A. True
    B. False

2. Which food would NOT be stored in the designated allergen special order food section?

    A. Wheat-free salad dressing.
    B. Gluten-free muffins.
    C. Shellfish and crab.
    D. Banana bread without nuts.

3. What item would be could NOT be stored with foods that contain Big 8 allergens?

    A. Gluten-free cookies
    B. Bananas and strawberries
    C. Molasses
    D. Deli ham and turkey

4. Which foods should be stored separately as allergen special order food?

    A. Whole grain bread
    B. Banana nut muffins
    C. Chocolate chip cookies
    D. Wheat-free brownies

5. Which items would be stored in an allergen special order section?

    A. Chicken and bacon.
    B. Milk and eggs.
    C. Gluten-free cookies.
    D. Whole wheat bread.

6. When cleaning allergen storage areas, you should:

    A. Work quickly.
    B. Use cloth rags.
    C. Clean thoroughly.
    D. Use bleach,

7. What should you use to clean allergen storage areas?

    A. Buckets and cloth towels
    B. Bleach
    C. Hot water and a sponge
    D. Spray bottles and disposable paper towels

8. **Why might an operation mark equipment as clean with time stamped stickers?**

    A. So employees know to use different equipment.
    B. Because it is safe for allergen special orders.
    C. Because it needs to be re-cleaned.
    D. There is no reason to do this.

9. **Careful cleaning of the kitchen can help prevent what?**

    A. Cross-contact
    B. Cross-contamination
    C. Both of the above
    D. None of the above

10. **True or false: In the kitchen it is usually too busy to make cleaning a priority.**

    A. True
    B. False

11. **Allergen special orders should be prepared:**

    A. In the same area as regular orders.
    B. With the same utensils as regular orders.
    C. Separately from regular orders.
    D. In the allergen special order zone only.

12. **True or False: Cleaning is extremely important in both the front and the back of the house.**

    A. True
    B. False

13. **If an allergen food protein is present on a piece of equipment, what happens to all the foods that touch that equipment?**

    A. There is no chance of cross-contact.
    B. Cross-contact will occur with all of the food.
    C. The food will have extra protein.
    D. The food will be very flavorful.

14. **What should you use to clean the kitchen and prep areas?**

    A. Spray bottles and paper towels
    B. Buckets and paper towels
    C. Spray bottles and cloth towels
    D. Buckets and cloth towels

15. **What is the risk in using regular cloths to clean?**

    A. There is no risk.
    B. Using regular cloths is the best way to clean.
    C. Food proteins can be spread around.
    D. Food proteins can be destroyed.

16. **Which answer is a physical boundary to prevent contact when cooking allergen special order food on a grill?**

 A. Saucepans
 B. Aluminum foil
 C. Cutting boards
 D. Frying pans

17. **True or false: It is okay to cook all foods in the same fryer.**

 A. True
 B. False

18. **What equipment cannot be shared by allergen special orders and regular orders?**

 A. Fryers
 B. Cutting Boards
 C. Grills
 D. Saucepans

19. **Which of the following are examples of equipment that cannot be entirely cleaned of allergens?**

 A. Waffle irons
 B. Toasters
 C. Colanders
 D. All of the above

20. **Choose the best policy for using utensils on allergen special orders.**

 A. Throw away utensils after contact with allergens.
 B. Throw away utensils after contact with regular orders.
 C. Use color-coded utensils.
 D. Use the same utensils for everything.

21. **What item of clothing should you replace before working on an allergen special order?**

 A. Your hat
 B. Your apron
 C. Your shirt
 D. Your entire outfit

22. **Before making an allergen special order you need to:**

 A. Wash your hands.
 B. Replace your gloves.
 C. Use hand sanitizer.
 D. Answers **A** and **B**

Orders

1. Should you need to wipe something down while preparing an allergen special order, you should use:

    A. A disposable paper towel.
    B. A clean cloth towel.
    C. Your apron.
    D. Your hand.

2. Before making the allergen special order, you should confirm:

    A. The correct recipe.
    B. The correct allergen special order.
    C. The correct ingredients.
    D. All of the above.

3. Why would it be a good idea to place a cover over a plate for a guest with a food allergy?

    A. To make it more presentable to the guest.
    B. To hide that it is an allergen special order.
    C. To prevent cross-contact.
    D. To confuse servers.

4. What might indicate that a plate is an allergen special order?

    A. Extra utensils.
    B. Extra garnishes.
    C. A gluten-free muffin.
    D. A colored sticker.

5. Which is NOT a way to visually indicate that a plate is an allergen special order?

    A. Adding a colored toothpick.
    B. Telling the server it is an allergen special order.
    C. Putting a cover over the plate.
    D. Double plating.

6. Which is NOT an example of how an allergen special order can be compromised right before it is taken to the guest?

    A. Not touching the plate.
    B. Adding a sprinkle of cheese.
    C. Adding croutons.
    D. Stacking plates to take the order to the guest's table.

7. Preventing cross-contact is the top priority, so what in the kitchen MUST be clean?

    A. Aprons
    B. Equipment
    C. Everything
    D. Cutting boards

8. **Since food proteins can be transferred on your skin, _____ is important.**

> A. Clean clothes
> B. Washing hands
> C. Washing utensils
> D. Clean equipment

9. **When there is a designated person to assist a guest with a food allergy, what is that person's job?**

> A. To take the guest's order.
> B. To add garnishes before serving the order.
> C. To take the guest's order, communicate it to the chef, and take the correct plate to the right guest without any cross-contact.
> D. To take the guest's order, cook the order; add appropriate garnishes, sides, and sauces; and take the correct plate to the right guest without any cross-contact.

10. **What information should a server include on the ticket of a guest with a food allergy?**

> A. The time the order was made
> B. The guest's name
> C. The number of people in the party
> D. The date

11. **Who does the server need to tell about an allergen special order?**

> A. The entire staff
> B. The manager
> C. The hosts
> D. The chef

12. **Which of the following is a system for identifying allergen special orders?**

> A. A color-coded plate system
> B. Assigning letters randomly
> C. Using any color plate
> D. Not adding garnishes

13. **Who on the staff needs to understand the policy about handling allergen special orders?**

> A. Servers only
> B. Everyone
> C. Front of the house staff
> D. Back of the house staff

14. **True or False: Confirming an allergen special order meal at pickup is mandatory.**

> A. True
> B. False

15. **What should the person delivering the allergen special order do at pickup?**

    A. Chat with the chef about the order.
    B. Add garnishes and sauces.
    C. Confirm that it is the allergen special order.
    D. Find the original server to deliver the allergen special order.

16. **Before serving an allergen special order to the guest, what can be done to prevent cross-contact?**

    A. Allowing the food to cool first.
    B. Adding extra garnishes.
    C. Not adding garnishes.
    D. Adding sides to the dish.

17. **Who is the best person to deliver a meal to a guest with food allergies?**

    A. The manager.
    B. The designated person.
    C. The chef.
    D. The server.

18. **True or False: It is okay to stack plates beside or on top of an allergen special order when delivering them to the guest's table.**

    A. True
    B. False

19. **Which of the following happens first?**

    A. The kitchen prepares the allergen special order and plates it on a red allergen plate.
    B. The server asks the table whether they enjoyed their meal.
    C. The designated person adds garnishes and sauces.
    D. The manager serves the order to the guest.

20. **If cross-contact occurs and is caught by staff before the dish goes to the guest, what should be done about it?**

    A. The manager should be contacted immediately.
    B. The chef should be contacted immediately.
    C. Depending on the severity of the contact, the food may be okay to serve to the guest.
    D. The food should be discarded and remade.

21. **In the case of an allergic reaction emergency, employees should:**

    A. Wait for someone to do something.
    B. Call 911.
    C. Get out of the way by going home.
    D. Shout loudly over the commotion.

Policies

1. When is communication between the service staff and a guest with food allergy important?

    A. When the guest has a serious allergy.
    B. If the guest insists on an allergen-free meal.
    C. Always.
    D. Communication between the service staff and guests is not important.

2. It is essential for front of house staff to know the ingredients in all menu items. Which of the following are appropriate ways to communicate this information to a guest?

    A. Every server makes it up as they go.
    B. By listing them vocally.
    C. Showing food labels.
    D. Answers **B** and **C.**

3. Who in the operation needs to understand the policies and procedures for guests with food allergies?

    A. Management.
    B. Servers and hosts.
    C. Chef.
    D. All employees.

4. When do a guest's food allergies become a priority?

    A. Before a guest even walks through the door.
    B. The moment a guest identifies they have a food allergy.
    C. The moment a guest places an allergen special order.
    D. As their order is being prepared on identifying plates.

5. Which of the following is the best way to serve guests with food allergies?

    A. Special menus based on common food allergies.
    B. Menus that include visual markers identifying common food allergies.
    C. Charts that show which allergens are in each menu item.
    D. All of the above.

6. Why is it important to tailor menus to guests with food allergies?

    A. It is not important to tailor menus to guests with food allergies.
    B. So you don't have to answer allergy questions about the menu.
    C. So that guests are fully informed and served safely.
    D. Because it makes the menu more colorful.

7. True or False: Each server should create their own policies on serving guests with food allergies based on what works best for them.

    A. True
    B. False

8. **Select the best answer. When a restaurant has a "secret recipe" food item, the server should:**

    A. Simply inform the guest that a list of ingredients for that item is unavailable.
    B. Refuse to disclose potential allergens in that item.
    C. List any allergen ingredients.
    D. Reveal the entire recipe and ingredient list.

9. **Before seating a guest with a food allergy, a server should:**

    A. Always ask them if they are having a nice day.
    B. Take notes on their specific allergies for the chef.
    C. Use hand sanitizer.
    D. Clean their table again.

10. **When seating guests with food allergies extra precautions are needed; for example:**

    A. Letting guests know their table has been cleaned and sanitized again.
    B. Replacing menus and utensils.
    C. All of the above.
    D. None of the above.

11. **When should laminated menus be cleaned?**

    A. When an employee notices they are looking dirty.
    B. Since they are laminated, they don't need to be cleaned.
    C. Before each new guest uses one.
    D. On a regular basis and when requested.

Receiving and Storage

1. True or False: Cross-contact can occur during shipping.

    A. True
    B. False

2. Once cross-contact has occurred during shipping, nothing can get the allergens off. The best course of action with products that have been exposed to cross-contact is:

    A. To fully cook those items.
    B. To keep those items refrigerated.
    C. To reject some or all of the products.
    D. There is nothing you can do.

3. While receiving a shipment, Lauren realizes the meat products have come into contact with a cheese product. What should Lauren do?

    A. Hope cross-contact did not occur.
    B. Reject some or all of the products.
    C. Ask her coworkers what they think she should do.
    D. She doesn't need to do anything.

4. What is an example of cross-contact during shipping?

    A. Bags of grain touching whole wheat flour.
    B. Milk products put next to cheese products.
    C. Peanuts packaged in an airtight container.
    D. Soymilk leaking onto flour.

5. Which is NOT an example of cross-contact during shipping?

    A. Milk products leaking into soy products.
    B. Tree nuts packaged beside almonds.
    C. Gluten-free mixes touching regular grains.
    D. Meat products touching dairy products.

6. Which products should not be next to each other during shipping?

    A. Fruits and vegetables
    B. Flour and baked goods
    C. Soy and milk products
    D. Chicken and beef

7. Soymilk has spilled onto several other products during shipping. Under what circumstances should these products be rejected and returned to the manufacturer?

    A. When a lot of soymilk has been spilt.
    B. Why your operation serves a lot of guests with milk allergies.
    C. These products should always be rejected because of cross-contact.
    D. These products do not need to be rejected because of cross-contact.

8. **Which two products are not okay to be shipped beside each other?**

    A. Skim milk and bleu cheese
    B. Lobster and crab
    C. Butter and peanut butter
    D. Gluten-free products

9. **Which represents the biggest risk?**

    A. Losing product during shipping.
    B. Losing paperwork.
    C. Spilling drinks.
    D. Receiving the wrong food in a shipment.

10. **How can you confirm that a delivery is correct?**

    A. Asking your coworkers.
    B. Making an educated guess.
    C. Comparing the delivery to its purchase order.
    D. Comparing the delivery to ingredients in popular recipes.

11. **When suppliers send similar substitute items to replace items they are out of, be sure to check the:**

    A. Food label
    B. Purchase order
    C. Delivery slip
    D. Recipe

12. **It is important to check the food labels of any substituted items in a delivery because,**

    A. They might not be up to the chef's standard.
    B. They may contain allergens.
    C. They may not contain allergens.
    D. They may have too many ingredients.

13. **True or False: Bread has wheat and gluten allergens, so it needs to be stored safely in a designated area.**

    A. True
    B. False

14. **True or False: One risk of egg deliveries is broken eggs spilling on other products.**

    A. True
    B. False

15. **Why is it important to reject products that have experienced cross-contact with allergens?**

    A. They put your guests at risk.
    B. The FDA demands it.
    C. It costs the operation money.
    D. It is not important.

16. **True or False: When suppliers substitute one product for another they make sure the products are the same in every way so no additional checking is needed.**

> A. True
> B. False

17. **A substituted product from a supplier lists "Contains: Milk and Wheat" on the label, while the original product did not. Why is this a problem?**

> A. It is not a problem.
> B. Because the new product contains allergens.
> C. Because the new product does not contain allergens.
> D. Because the new product may not taste the same.

18. **True or False: A substituted product from a supplier that contains no additional allergens is an adequate substitution for a guest with allergies.**

> A. True
> B. False

19. **True or False: Once food is in storage, it is not at risk for cross-contact.**

> A. True
> B. False

20. **Which of the following is not a good rule regarding food storage?**

> A. Keep foods in sealed containers.
> B. Clearly label all foods.
> C. Keep foods with allergens in separate containers.
> D. Keep allergen special order foods and regular foods together.

Service

1. Choose the correct statement about cross-contact.

    A. Small amounts of cross-contact are acceptable.
    B. Cross-contact can be prevented by putting sauces on separate plates.
    C. Cross-contact can be prevented by stacking plates on top of each other.
    D. Cross-contact can be prevented by serving extremely hot food.

2. True or False.: There is little chance of cross-contact once the dish leaves the kitchen.

    A. True
    B. False

3. Which statement contains an error?

    A. Refrain from adding garnishes to an allergen special order.
    B. Any amount of cross-contact is enough to trigger an allergic reaction.
    C. Cross-contact can be prevented by completely cooking food.
    D. Carry the dish by hand to the guest.

4. During an emergency, what could an employee do to help the situation?

    A. Wait outside to signal the ambulance.
    B. Serve everyone a hot drink.
    C. Hide in the break room.
    D. Nothing.

5. Jose is the designated person serving a dairy-free meal to a guest. At pickup he adds garnishes to all dishes for the table and carries them all out to the table. What error has Jose made?

    A. He added garnishes to an allergen special order.
    B. He carried the allergen order with other plates risking cross-contact.
    C. He didn't wash his hands immediately before carrying the plates.
    D. Answers **A** and **B**.

6. Which of the following would not prevent cross-contact when serving food?

    A. Carrying multiple plates.
    B. Putting salad dressing on a separate plate.
    C. Putting French fries on a separate plate.
    D. Confirming the allergen special order.

7. Ricky confirms that the dish is the allergen special order, then carries it directly to the guest. What mistake has Ricky made?

    A. Bothering the kitchen staff by asking about the order.
    B. Forgetting to add garnishes.
    C. Not letting the food cool first.
    D. Ricky did not make a mistake.

8. **How might a server recognize an allergen special order?**

    A. The dish with extra bread.
    B. The dish on a red plate.
    C. The dish with no cheese.
    D. There are no ways to visually identify an allergen special order.

9. **Which is the last step of the following?**

    A. Telling the chef about the allergen special order.
    B. Adding sauces or garnishes.
    C. Confirming the allergen special order.
    D. Taking the guest's order.

10. **What is a "May Contain" statement?**

    A. A complete list of ingredients.
    B. A list of Big 8 allergens that are present in the product.
    C. A statement disclosing that there might be small amounts of a food allergen in the product.
    D. A statement telling people with food allergies to eat at their own risk.

11. **True or False: Manufacturers are legally required to list "May Contain" statements.**

    A. True
    B. False

12. **True or False: All guests with food allergies know to order off the menu because self-service stations offer too many potential hazards.**

    A. True
    B. False

13. **Which of the following is a way to improve a self-service station?**

    A. Adding new food directly into existing containers.
    B. Making items easy to reach.
    C. Placing utensils at a nearby station.
    D. Removing sneeze guards.

14. **Which of the following are good rules for maintaining a self-service station?**

    A. Including as many packaged products as possible.
    B. Designating utensils for each item.
    C. Answers **A** and **B.**
    D. None of the above.

15. **Which example illustrates best practice for a self-service station?**

    A. Accurate signage.
    B. Placing items with allergens away from those without.
    C. Answers **A** and **B**.
    D. None of the above.

16. **When Jamie adds new food into an existing container, which rule is she breaking?**

A. Always clean the self service station before adding new food.
B. Never add new food near other items with allergens.
C. Designate utensils for each self-service item.
D. Do not mix new food with old food.

17. **Which of the following is a way to prevent cross-contact?**

A. Using the same utensil for every item.
B. Using dedicated cleaning equipment.
C. Opening all packaged products.
D. Placing breads, salad dressings, and condiments on a separate station.

18. **True or False: It is more important to keep a self-service station clean and maintained than a work station.**

A. True
B. False

19. **Mark has a wheat allergy. When he uses the tongs used for muffins for hard-boiled eggs, what is this an example of?**

A. Cross-Contamination
B. Cross-Contact
C. Condiment Contact
D. None of the above

20. **True or False: Packaged foods on a self service station need to be labeled for allergens.**

A. True
B. False

21. **When a table requests drink refills and a breadbasket refill, their server should:**

A. Let them refill these items themselves.
B. Refill drinks from a pitcher and bring a new breadbasket.
C. Replace drinks and breadbasket.
D. Replace drinks and refill the existing breadbasket.

Answers

Allergens & Intolerances

1. **Answer: C -** Food Allergy Research and Education estimates that 15 million Americans have food allergies

Organizations like Food Allergy Research and Education are being created to support the millions of Americans who have food allergies. The number of people with food allergies is still growing without definitive research about why. Due to the large number of people who experience allergies, the fact that mainly children are affected, and that allergies can be fatal, food allergies are a serious subject.

2. **Answer: B -** The number of people suffering from allergies is NOT decreasing over time.

For reasons that researchers do not understand, the number of people experiencing food allergies is growing. Of these, the largest population affected is children. This is a global phenomenon and the European Academy of Allergy and Clinical Immunology is leading the way for research in Europe, as 17 million Europeans suffer from allergies.

3. **Answer: C -** Food allergies are when the immune system mistakenly labels a harmless protein as toxic, then attacks it.

The immune system's job is to protect the body from foreign pathogens. During an allergic reaction, the immune system believes that a harmless food protein, or allergen, is toxic to the body and attempts to destroy it.

4. **Answer: B -** Food allergies are more than just inconvenient; they can be life-threatening

In a person with a food allergy, some foods can trigger a severe form of allergic reaction called anaphylaxis. When someone goes into anaphylaxis, they require emergency medical care, including a shot of a medication called Epinephrine. Without immediate treatment, anaphylaxis can result in death.

5. **Answer: A -** Food allergies can be serious enough to send a person to the emergency room

When a person with food allergies experiences anaphylaxis, a potentially fatal reaction to an allergen, 911 should be called immediately. Young adults and people who have asthma and/or food allergies are particularly at risk of death from anaphylaxis.

6. **Answer: C -** There are approximately 200,000 food related emergency room visits per year.

This statistic speaks to the magnitude of people seriously affected by food allergies, and it doesn't even include the 300,000 ambulatory visits for children alone. Without immediate emergency treatment, food allergies can cause fatalities.

7. **Answer: A -** Edamame is an example of a "Big 8" food allergy.

The "Big 8" food allergens are milk, eggs, peanuts, tree nuts, shellfish, wheat, fish and soy. Edamame is a dish of soybeans still in the pod. It is possible to be allergic to any food, including chicken and spinach, but strawberries are a fairly common allergen.

8. **Answer: C -** While the "big 8" foods account for 90% of all food allergies, there are still more than 160 known food allergens. Corn, meat, seeds and fruit are a few examples of non-Big 8 foods.

9. **Answer: C -** Shrimp, whole-wheat bread, and milk are examples of "Big 8" allergens.

Shellfish (like shrimp), wheat products, and milk are some of the most common allergies. The "Big 8" also includes eggs, soybeans, fish, tree nuts, and peanuts. These foods account for 90% of all allergic reactions.

10. **Answer: D -** Children experience the highest rates of food allergies.

Children's immune systems are more reactive to allergens. While all of the "Big 8" allergens are common triggers, peanuts are the most frequent. It is possible for children to outgrow some food allergies; however peanuts, shellfish, and tree nuts are usually lifelong allergies.

11. **Answer: B -** Jillian should call 911.

Having a severe allergy to peanuts puts Jillian at high risk for anaphylaxis. Anaphylaxis is a severe form of allergic reaction that requires immediate medical attention or it could be fatal.

12. **Answer: D-** The "Big 8" are responsible for 90% of all allergic reactions.

The "Big 8" are wheat, peanuts, tree nuts, shellfish, finned fish, soy beans, milk, and eggs. As these foods are responsible for most allergic reactions, any processed food in the United States must declare them on the label. Peanuts and seafood are the most likely to cause anaphylaxis, require hospitalization, or result in death.

13. **Answer: C -** An umbrella term for adverse food reactions, including allergies and intolerances, is food sensitivities.

There are a lot of important vocabulary words when it comes to food allergies. A blanket term to cover adverse reactions to foods, allergies, and intolerances is food sensitivities.

14. **Answer: D -** Neither dairy allergy or celiac disease are examples of a food intolerance.

A food intolerance is unlike an allergy because it does not affect the immune system. While food intolerances do have some similar symptoms as a food allergy, they are much less severe and cannot result in anaphylaxis. Food intolerances are often uncomfortable, but not fatal.

15. **Answer: D -** An immune system reaction to dairy is an example of a food allergy.

A dairy allergy is an overreaction of the immune system to the proteins found in milk. When only the digestive system is involved, this is known as lactose intolerance and the affected person will experience digestive issues.

16. **Answer: B -** When George's immune system reacts to ice cream, it is an example of a dairy allergy.

The differentiating factor between lactose intolerance and a true dairy allergy is whether or not the immune system is involved. Lactose intolerance means the body is missing the lactose enzyme and cannot break down the sugar found in dairy products. George's immune system, on the other hand, overreacts to the protein in dairy.

17. **Answer: C -** Ellie's digestive upset and discomfort can best be described as a soy intolerance.

Discomfort in the digestive tract is best described as an in tolerance unless there are also more severe symptoms like hives, reddening of the skin, nasal congestion, swelling, or trouble swallowing. These indicate a reaction by the immune system instead of just the digestive tract.

18. **Answer: D -** Gluten is found in wheat, rye, and barley.

A wheat allergy can cause a large problem for an individual when you consider that it is the most prominent grain product in America. Examples of foods containing wheat are pasta, bread crumbs, and couscous.

19. **Answer: A -** A Peanut allergy can be life threatening.

Even small amounts of peanut can trigger an allergic reaction. Sometimes just touching a peanut or peanut residue off of a surface can trigger a reaction. This is especially dangerous if someone with a peanut allergy casually touches a peanut, then touches their eyes, nose, or mouth.

20. **Answer: A -** Eating wheat would trigger symptoms in a person with Celiac Disease.

For a person with Celiac Disease, the only treatment is completely avoiding gluten, which is found in wheat, rye, and barley. Whenever gluten is consumed, it triggers a reaction in the body that damages the small intestine. This means food cannot be absorbed and a person can stay malnourished no matter how much they eat.

21. **Answer: C -** Celiac disease is an example of an autoimmune disease.

For someone with Celiac Disease, eating gluten causes the immune system to mistakenly attack the body's healthy tissues. Therefore Celiac Disease is not the same as digestive disturbance due to gluten, or gluten intolerance. Also, it is not an allergy because the immune system is not attacking the protein in ingested food.

22. **Answer: B -** There is no cure for Celiac Disease.

No cure for Celiac Disease has been discovered yet so the best option is a diet with absolutely no gluten. Celiac Disease is an autoimmune disease triggered by eating gluten.

23. **Answer: B -** There is no cure for a food allergy.

Since there is no cure for a food allergy, the only therapy is to avoid the offending food. Epinephrine is a very useful medication for emergency allergic reactions that would otherwise result in death. Epinephrine is a self-administered injection of adrenaline, and is extremely effective when used right away.

24. **Answer: D -** Symptoms of an allergic reaction can occur immediately or take several hours to appear.

The most severe reactions happen immediately or within minutes of exposure. The severity of a person's allergic reaction depends on their individual genetics and the amount of allergen ingested.

25. **Answer: A -** Hives are a symptom of allergic reaction.

Hives are considered a mild symptom of an allergic reaction and are not fatal. These red, itchy, swollen patches of skin can break out anywhere on the body.

26. **Answer: C -** Migraines are NOT a symptom of an allergic reaction.

Symptoms of an allergic reaction can be as mild as an odd taste in the mouth or as severe as anaphylaxis. Itchy rashes, hives, abdominal pain, and swelling are all examples of mild allergy symptoms.

27. **Answer: C -** When a guest places a special order due to an allergy, they are trusting you with their health and safety.

Food allergies range from mild to life threatening, so it always important be vigilant about them. If a guest goes into anaphylaxis because of exposure to an allergen, their life could be in danger.

28. **Answer: C -** Laura might have ingested Lobster, which is shellfish.

While all of the answers represent allergens from the "Big 8," only lobster falls into the category of either shellfish or tree nuts. Examples of tree nuts include cashews, Brazil nuts, almonds, and walnuts. Examples of shellfish include shrimp, crab, and mollusks. Peanuts are not to be confused with tree nuts, as they are a legume.

29. **Answer: C -** Trevor might experience swelling.

Swelling is a serious symptom of a food allergy that can be fatal. Swelling of the mouth and through can cause trouble swallowing and breathing. A serious symptom like swelling could be a sign of anaphylaxis, which requires emergency medical attention.

30. **Answer: C -** Diarrhea and wheezing are also common symptoms of an allergic reaction.

An allergic reaction can affect the entire body, including the skin, lungs, and digestive tract. While hives and digestive distress are mild symptoms, wheezing could mean obstructed breathing and requires medical attention.

31. **Answer: D -** During an allergic reaction there can be swelling of the hands, feet, and face.

Swelling is an allergic reaction symptom that can occur anywhere in the body. In its most serious form, swelling of the mouth and throat can obstruct breathing or cause trouble swallowing.

32. **Answer: A -** Monica's nausea, diarrhea, and abdominal pain could mean she is experiencing lactose intolerance.

A milk allergy may have symptoms like hives, itching, swelling, and wheezing. However, lactose intolerance is not the same as an allergy because it does not affect the immune system. By lacking the enzyme "lactase," a lactose intolerant person is unable to break down the sugar found in dairy products.

Food Handling

1. **Answer: C -** It is the designated person's job to take the guest's order, communicate it to the chef, and take the correct plate to the right guest without cross-contact.

The goal of the designated person is to make sure a guest with a food allergy gets the correct order. By checking each step in the process, it is much more likely that one designated person will get the order correct than it would be if multiple employees were involved.

2. **Answer: B -** A server should include the name of the guest with a food allergy on the ticket.

In circumstances where the server that takes the order is not the person delivering it to a guest, having the guest's name ensures the person gets their correct meal. Another way to identify the correct allergen special order is a color-coding system where allergen orders are put on a different colored plate.

3. **Answer: D -** The server needs to tell the chef about an allergen special order.

To ensure that the order is delivered to the guest correctly, the person who took the order must communicate it directly to the chef. It is then up to the chef to prepare the meal without cross-contact.

4. **Answer: A -** A color-coded plate system is a way to identify allergen special orders

Color-coding is a fast and decisive way to identify allergen special orders. This could mean using plates, toothpicks, or straws as long as there is a universal meaning for the identifiers used.

5. **Answer: B -** Everyone on the staff needs to understand the policy about handling allergen special orders.

All staff members must understand this procedure so that no mistakes are made along the way.

6. **Answer: A -** Confirming an allergen special order meal at pickup is mandatory.

Pickup is the last chance to confirm that an order is correct before it is delivered to the guest. The person delivering the order should verbally confirm the meal, then carry it by hand to the guest.

7. **Answer: C -** At pickup, the person delivering the allergen special order should confirm that it is the correct meal.

Verbally confirming that this is an allergen special order is the final check before serving an order to a guest. The order should then be delivered by hand to the right guest.

8. **Answer: C -** Not adding garnishes to an allergen special order can prevent cross-contact.

An allergen special order should be delivered by hand to the guest so that there are no opportunities for cross-contact. Serving sauces and sides on separate dishes are additional ways to prevent cross-contact.

9. **Answer: B -** The designated person is the best option to deliver a meal to a guest with food allergies.

Having the designated person deliver the food reduces the chance of cross-contact. It ensures that the dish will be delivered to the right guest without additional garnishes or sauces being added.

10. **Answer: B -** It is NOT okay to stack plates beside or on top of an allergen special order when delivering them to the guest's table.

Allergen special orders should be delivered by hand to the guest. Stacking plates or spilling other foods on this order are easy ways for cross-contact to occur. Try to keep an allergen special order separate from all other foods.

11. **Answer: A -** The first event is the kitchen preparing the allergen special order and plating it on a red allergen plate.

Preparing the allergen special order is the first step out of the options listed. Using a red-colored plate to signify an allergen special order is an effective way to differentiate the dish.

12. **Answer: D -** If cross-contact occurs, the food should be discarded and remade.

Any amount of cross-contact could transfer enough food protein to trigger an allergic reaction. In all circumstances, the guest's safety comes before the inconvenience of recooking their order.

13. **Answer: B -** In the case of an allergic reaction, emergency employees should call 911.

During anaphylaxis, emergency medical attention is needed and 911 should be called right away. Then employees can wait outside to signal to the ambulance where help is needed.

14. **Answer: C -** Cross-contact refers to when two foods come into contact so that their proteins mix.

A small amount is sufficient for cross-contact to occur and usually the amounts are small enough that they cannot be seen. After cross-contact, each food has small amounts of the other food in it.

15. **Answer: B -** Large amounts of two different foods are NOT needed for cross-contact to occur.

Most frequently the amounts of food are so small that they cannot be seen by the naked eye. Even such small amounts are enough to trigger an allergic reaction.

16. **Answer: A -** Putting cheese on a sandwich is an example of cross-contact.

Cross-contact can be either direct or indirect. Putting cheese on a sandwich is an example of direct cross-contamination.

17. **Answer: B -** Cross-contact and cross-contamination are separate things.

These two terms are still frequently misused or used interchangeably. Cross-contamination is the common cause of foodborne illnesses. Cross-contact is when two foods touch and mix proteins. In this way, cross-contact may cause allergens to be passed between foods.

18. **Answer: A -** Cross-contamination occurs when disease-causing organisms are transferred between two foods.

19. **Answer: C -** Cross-contamination can cause foodborne illness.

20. **Answer: B -** Using cleaner, rinse, and sanitizer spray bottles with disposable paper towels is the correct cleaning procedure.

21. **Answer: A -** Handling an allergen while preparing food is an example of cross-contact.

22. **Answer: D -** Food proteins can be found on surfaces, clothing, and hands.

23. **Answer: A -** Cooking foods to the right temperature can prevent foodborne illness.

24. **Answer: A -** Cross-contact involves the transfer of proteins, while cross-contamination involves the transfer of disease-causing organisms.

25. **Answer: C -** Using clean utensils and washing hands would help prevent cross-contact.

Food Labels

1. **Answer: A -** "This product does not contain" is NOT an example of a "May Contain" statement.

"May Contain" statements are optional lists by manufacturers listing foods that may be found in trace amounts. Statements listing what a product does NOT contain are not considered "May Contain" statements.

2. **Answer: B -** Legally, food labels are required to list the Big 8 allergens.

As the Big 8 allergens account for 90% of all food allergies, the FDA requires that they or any ingredient derived from them be listed on the label. Some manufacturers go above this to list items the product may contain, but they are not legally obligated to do so.

3. **Answer: A -** If peanuts are listed in the ingredients list a manufacturer is NOT required to list it with the ingredients in a "Contains" list.

Legally, manufacturers have three ways to list potential allergens in foods. The allergens must be listed either in the product's ingredient list, in parentheses beside an item in the ingredient list, or in a list of Big 8 allergens called the "Contains" list.

4. **Answer: D -** Chefs, cooks, and receiving staff regularly use food label reading skills.

Whenever a chef creates a recipe he must refer to the ingredient list. Cooks must be familiar with allergens because they regularly prepare orders for guests with food allergies. The receiving staff ensures that products including the Big 8 are known to the customer.

5. **Answer: A -** Casein and cream are other names for milk.

Guest with food allergies need to avoid foods that contain "milk" or foods derived from milk. Examples one might see on a food label include butter, curds, lactose, whey, and yogurt.

6. **Answer: B -** Miso and edamame are other names for soy.

The soybean is a member of the legume family, which also includes lentils, beans, peas, and peanuts. Having a soy allergy does not make someone more likely to be allergic to peanuts as well. Other names for soy on food labels include soybean, tempeh, tofu, and soy sauce.

7. **Answer: A -** Filbert and almonds may be listed on a food label and they are tree nuts.

A guest with a tree nut allergy has a high chance of being allergic to several types of tree nut. These may include hazelnuts, cashews, almonds, Brazil nuts, pistachios, and walnuts. Frequently, a guest with a tree nut allergy must also avoid peanuts due to cross-contact that could occur during manufacturing and processing.

8. **Answer: D -** Legally, Big 8 allergens must be listed in the "Contains" list of food packages.

Whenever a Big 8 allergen is an ingredient in a product, it must be listed on the label. Even a trace amount from flavoring, coloring, or spices merits being on the label. Some manufactures take an extra step to list what Big 8 items may be in the product accidentally.

9. **Answer: B -** Keeping all allergens out of the kitchen from the start is a good way to keep guests safe.

The only way for someone with a food allergy to avoid symptoms is by completely avoiding the offending food at all times. There is no cure that will make their allergen safe to eat. It may be possible to keep some allergens out of your operation altogether, but that isn't always possible, so the allergens must be kept separately.

10. **Answer: A -** Ordering from specialty suppliers that cater to allergen special orders can keep allergens out of your kitchen.

With the growing number of people with food allergies, the need for suppliers who cater to guests with allergies is also growing. Ordering from a specialty supplier is another way to ensure the product you receive has not experienced cross-contact.

Kitchen and Prep

1. **Answer: A -** A great way to store allergen special order foods is in a designated area for allergen-free foods.

Keeping a storage section for foods without the Big 8 as ingredients reduces the risk of cross-contact. Keeping foods stored in an organized way protects your guest's health.

2. **Answer: C -** Shellfish and crab would not be stored in the designated allergen special order food section.

Shellfish allergies tend to be one of the most severe allergies. Cross-contact between shellfish and other products at your operation could result in anaphylaxis for an unsuspecting guest.

3. **Answer: A -** Gluten-free cookies could NOT be stored with foods that contain the Big 8 allergens.

Ideally, foods for allergen special orders should be stored away from regular foods. Cross-contact could expose gluten, wheat, or other allergens to gluten-free foods.

4. **Answer: D -** Wheat-free brownies should be stored separately as allergen special order food.

Separating foods specifically for allergen special orders protects your guests. Cross-contact with other baked goods could expose wheat-free brownies to dairy, tree nuts, or wheat.

5. **Answer: C -** Gluten-free cookies would be stored in an allergen special order section.

Ideally, foods that do not contain the Big 8 should be stored separately. Cross-contact is a risk even when foods are in storage and any contact makes the foods unsafe for your guests.

6. **Answer: C -** Clean allergen storage areas thoroughly.

Cleaning is important everywhere in your operation because cross-contact and cross-contamination can happen anywhere. Use spray bottles of cleaner, rinse, and sanitizer with disposable paper towels.

7. **Answer: D -** When you clean allergen storage areas use spray bottles and disposable paper towels.

Traditional buckets and cloth towels spread food proteins across surfaces. Food proteins can stay on the cloth or the bucket itself and be carried all over the kitchen.

8. **Answer: B -** An operation might mark equipment as clean with time stamped stickers to signal that it is safe for allergen special orders.

If equipment is shared between regular and allergen special orders, proper equipment cleaning is key. While some equipment, like a waffle iron, cannot be used for both regular orders and allergen special orders, other equipment can be made safe through thorough cleaning and sanitizing.

9. **Answer: C -** Careful cleaning of the kitchen can help prevent cross-contact and cross-contamination.

Cross-contact is when two foods mix proteins and small amounts of each food are found in the other. Cross-contamination is the spread of disease-causing organisms. These can both be prevented with diligence and cleaning.

10. **Answer: B -** It is never too busy in the kitchen to make cleaning a priority.

Cleaning is the best defense against cross-contact and cross-contamination. Without it a guest with food allergies could be endangered

11. **Answer: C -** Allergen special orders should be prepared separately from regular orders.

Allergen special orders cannot be prepared with regular orders because of the risk of cross contamination. Any tools used for both kinds of orders, as well as the station the food is prepared on must be thoroughly cleaned.

12. **Answer: A -** Cleaning is extremely important in both the front and the back of the house.

Cross-contamination and cross-contact can be prevented with proper cleaning. This is why it is always a priority all over the operation.

13. **Answer: B -** When an allergen food protein is on a piece of equipment, cross-contact will occur with all of the food that touches that equipment.

Amounts of food small enough to be invisible are enough to trigger an allergic reaction. Any time equipment is used to prepare an allergen special order, it must be cleaned to remove lingering food proteins.

14. **Answer: A -** Use spray bottles and paper towels to clean the kitchen and prep areas.

Spray bottles of cleaner, rinse, and sanitizer with disposable paper towels are the preferred method of cleaning all over the operation. Traditional buckets with cloth towels spread food protein across the kitchen.

15. **Answer: C -** There is a risk of spreading food proteins around when using regular cloths.

Food proteins on regular cloths can be spread around the kitchen, increasing the risk of cross-contamination. This is why disposable cloths are preferable.

16. **Answer: B -** Aluminum foil is a physical boundary to prevent contact when cooking allergen special order food on a grill.

Aluminum foil prevents the allergen special order food from touching the grill. This way it can be on the grill at the same time as regular orders.

17. **Answer: B -** It is NOT okay to cook all foods in the same fryer.

The fryer is an example of equipment that cannot be shared between regular and allergen special orders. Any amount of allergen in the fryer could cause allergic reactions in guests. Other equipment that cannot be shared includes the waffle iron, colander, and meat slicer.

18. **Answer: A -** Fryers cannot be shared by allergen special orders and regular ones.

An allergen in the fryer would mean that all food coming out of the fryer would be cross-contacted with that allergen. An alternative frying method is having a pot of oil on the stove exclusively for allergen special orders.

19. **Answer: D -** Waffle irons, toasters, and colanders cannot be entirely cleaned of allergens.

These items could never be cleaned in a way that would make them 100% safe for allergen special orders. In many operations, this means there is a duplicate set of these items for allergen special orders.

20. **Answer: C -** Use color-coded utensils for allergen special orders.

When possible, having a second set of utensils that are color-coded for allergen special orders is ideal. In situations where this is not possible, utensils should be cleaned using the dishwasher.

21. **Answer: B -** Before working on an allergen special order you should replace your apron.

Food proteins can be transferred on equipment, utensils and fabrics. If you cannot change to a second apron, remove your apron before preparing the allergen special order.

22. **Answer: D -** Before making an allergen special order you need to wash your hands and replace your gloves.

Alcohol-based hand sanitizers are not effective at removing food proteins from skin. Thoroughly washing hands and replacing gloves are necessary to prevent cross-contact.

Orders

1. **Answer: A -** If you need to wipe something down while preparing an allergen special order, you should use a disposable paper towel.

2. **Answer: D -** Before making the order confirm the recipe, ingredients, and that you have the correct order.

It is important to confirm that you are preparing the correct recipe with allergen-free ingredients for the guest. When checking ingredients, read the food label to find out what allergens it contains.

3. **Answer: C -** It would be a good idea to place a cover over a plate for a guest with a food allergy to prevent cross-contact.

There are many ways to identify that a plate is an allergen special order. Any policy that is universally recognized by the staff is an adequate way to identify allergy special orders. Other examples include double plating and marking plates with stickers.

4. **Answer: D -** A plate might have a colored sticker to indicate it is an allergen special order.

Adding garnishes and sides onto the plate are examples of things not to do to an allergen special order because of cross-contact. Colored stickers, toothpick flags, and double plating are all ways to indicate an allergen special order.

5. **Answer: B -** Telling the server it is an allergen special order is NOT a way to visually indicate it.

Verbally telling the server the plate is an allergen special order is not a way to visually indicate it. Before the server delivers the plate to the guests, they should confirm with the kitchen staff that it is the allergen special order.

6. **Answer: A -** Not touching the plate is not an example of how an allergen special order can be compromised right before it is taken to the guest.

All garnishes should be skipped for an allergen special order. Also, anything additional for the plate should be plated separately. Stacking plates to deliver them to the guest could cause cross-contact with other dishes.

7. **Answer: C -** Since preventing cross-contact is the top priority, everything in the kitchen must be clean.

Food proteins can be on clothing, equipment, cutting boards, and everything else in the kitchen. Using designated cleaning supplies to clean, rinse, and sanitize with disposable paper towels is important.

8. **Answer: B -** Food proteins can be transferred on your skin, so washing your hands is important.

Hand sanitizers do not remove food proteins from skin. Only by thoroughly washing hands can cross-contact by skin be prevented.

9. **Answer: C -** It is the designated person's job to take the guest's order, communicate it to the chef, and take the correct plate to the right guest without cross-contact.

The goal of the designated person is to make sure a guest with a food allergy gets the correct order. By checking each step in the process, it is much more likely that one designated person will get the order correct than it would be if multiple employees were involved.

10. **Answer: B -** A server should include the name of the guest with a food allergy on the ticket.

In circumstances where the server that takes the order is not the person delivering it to a guest, having the guest's name ensures the person gets their correct meal. Another way to identify the correct allergen special order is a color-coding system where allergen orders are put on a different colored plate.

11. **Answer: D -** The server needs to tell the chef about an allergen special order.

To ensure that the order is delivered to the guest correctly, the person who took the order must communicate it directly to the chef. It is then up to the chef to prepare the meal without cross-contact.

12. **Answer: A -** A color-coded plate system is a way to identify allergen special orders

Color-coding is a fast and decisive way to identify allergen special orders. This could mean using plates, toothpicks, or straws as long as there is a universal meaning for the identifiers used.

13. **Answer: B -** Everyone on the staff needs to understand the policy about handling allergen special orders.

All staff members must understand this procedure so that no mistakes are made along the way.

14. **Answer: A -** Confirming an allergen special order meal at pickup is mandatory.

Pickup is the last chance to confirm that an order is correct before it is delivered to the guest. The person delivering the order should verbally confirm the meal, then carry it by hand to the guest.

15. **Answer: C -** At pickup, the person delivering the allergen special order should confirm that it is the correct meal.

Verbally confirming that this is an allergen special order is the final check before serving an order to a guest. The order should then be delivered by hand to the right guest.

16. **Answer: C -** Not adding garnishes to an allergen special order can prevent cross-contact.

An allergen special order should be delivered by hand to the guest so that there are no opportunities for cross-contact. Serving sauces and sides on separate dishes are additional ways to prevent cross-contact.

17. **Answer: B -** The designated person is the best option to deliver a meal to a guest with food allergies.

Having the designated person deliver the food reduces the chance of cross-contact. It ensures that the dish will be delivered to the right guest without additional garnishes or sauces being added.

18. **Answer: B -** It is NOT okay to stack plates beside or on top of an allergen special order when delivering them to the guest's table.

Allergen special orders should be delivered by hand to the guest. Stacking plates or spilling other foods on this order are easy ways for cross-contact to occur. Try to keep an allergen special order separate from all other foods.

19. **Answer: A -** The first event is the kitchen preparing the allergen special order and plating it on a red allergen plate.

Preparing the allergen special order is the first step out of the options listed. Using a red-colored plate to signify an allergen special order is an effective way to differentiate the dish.

20. **Answer: D -** If cross-contact occurs, the food should be discarded and remade.

Any amount of cross-contact could transfer enough food protein to trigger an allergic reaction. In all circumstances, the guest's safety comes before the inconvenience of recooking their order.

21. **Answer: B -** In the case of an allergic reaction, emergency employees should call 911.

During anaphylaxis, emergency medical attention is needed and 911 should be called right away. Then employees can wait outside to signal to the ambulance where help is needed.

Policies

1. **Answer: C -** Communication between the service staff and guest is always important.

2. **Answer: D -** Listing ingredients vocally and showing guest food labels are appropriate ways to communicate ingredients to guests.

3. **Answer: D -** All employees need to understand the policies and procedures for guests with food allergies

4. **Answer: A -** A guest's food allergies become a priority before they even walk through the door.

5. **Answer: D -** All of the above are the best ways serve guests with food allergies.

6. **Answer: C -** It is important to tailor menus to guests with food allergies so they are fully informed and served safely.

7. **Answer: B -** Servers should NOT create their own policies on serving guests with food allergies.

8. **Answer: C -** The server should list any allergen ingredients.

9. **Answer: D -** Before seating a guest with a food allergy, a server should clean their table again.

10. **Answer: C -** Replacing menus and utensils as well as cleaning the table again is needed for guests with food allergies.

11. **Answer: D -** Laminated menus should be cleaned on a regular basis and when requested.

Receiving and Storage

1. **Answer: A -** Cross-contact can occur during shipping.

When allergen specialty products are packaged carelessly, it is possible for foods to experience cross-contact before they reach your operation. Checking the condition of shipping containers and looking for possible spills is very important.

2. **Answer: C -** Once cross-contact has occurred during shipping, it is best to reject some or all of the products.

Foods that have experienced cross-contact can never be prepared or cooked to a point where they are safe for guests with food allergies. There are many specialty suppliers who cater to allergen-specific foods and would be able to deliver products that have not been compromised. If this is not an option at your operation, checking shipping containers and looking for spills is very important.

3. **Answer: B -** Lauren should reject some or all of the products exposed to cross-contact.

Cooking the meat to the recommended temperature will do nothing to reverse the effects of cross-contact. As the food will never be safe for guests with food allergies, the only course of action is to return it for acceptable product.

4. **Answer: D -** Soymilk leaking onto flour during shipping is an example of cross-contact.

In this example, soymilk and flour are both potential triggers. Small amounts of soy in the flour could trigger someone with a soy allergy. Likewise, wheat in the soy could trigger someone with a wheat allergy.

5. **Answer: B -** Tree nuts packaged beside almonds is not an example of cross-contact during shipping.

Cross-contact occurs when two foods touch and their proteins mix. This can happen when products are located close together or when there is a spill during shipping. The only course of action is to reject some or all of the product.

6. **Answer: C -** Soy and milk products should not be next to each other during shipping.

When small amounts of soy and milk mix proteins, cross-contact has occurred. It is important to look for damaged shipping containers or evidence of spillage to prevent these products from entering your operation.

7. **Answer: C -** Under these circumstances, the products should always be rejected because of cross-contact.

Any products exposed to soy will not trigger a guest with a soy allergy. To ensure the safety of your guests it is best to reject food that is not safe for them to eat.

8. **Answer: C -** Butter and peanut butter are not okay to be shipped beside each other.

Both butter and peanut butter are allergens on their own. After mixing proteins, someone eating the butter could experience an allergic reaction to peanuts and vice versa.

9. **Answer: D -** Receiving the wrong food in a shipment represents the biggest risk.

Chefs and cooks are prepared to make allergen special orders based on the knowledge of the products they have to cook with. When a supplier sends a substitute or incorrect product, it could contain allergens that the kitchen passes to the guest.

10. **Answer: C** - Comparing the delivery to its purchase order will confirm that a delivery is correct.

Checking the purchase order ensures that your operation has received the right amount of the right products. Unknowingly receiving an incorrect or substitute product could introduce allergies into your operation.

11. **Answer: A -** When suppliers send similar substitute items to replace items they are out of, be sure to check the food labels.

Receiving substitute products without reading the food label could introduce allergens into your operation. Just because a supplier deems a product to be an acceptable substitute does not mean that it contains the same ingredients.

12. **Answer: B -** It is important to check the food labels of any substituted items in a delivery because they may contain allergens.

Substitute products from a supplier are similar products, but do not necessarily have the same ingredients or allergens. Receiving staff must check these at delivery to make sure allergens are not introduced to the organization.

13. **Answer: A -** Bread has wheat and gluten allergens, so it needs to be stored safely in a designated area.

Many operations have designated areas for foods with and without Big 8 food allergens. Keeping bread away from products used for guests with food allergies means preventing cross-contact.

14. **Answer: A -** One risk of egg deliveries is broken eggs spilling on other products.

Cross-contact can occur during shipping. Checking the security of shipping boxes and identifying leaks are a part of keeping your guests safe.

15. **Answer: A -** It is important to reject products that have experienced cross-contact with allergens because they put your guests at risk.

Any amount of cross-contact is enough to trigger a reaction in a guest with allergies. There is no way to take food that has experienced cross-contact and make it safe for guests with allergies to eat.

16. **Answer: B -** When suppliers substitute one product for another they do NOT make sure the products are the same in every way, so additional checking is needed.

Different brands of the same product can contain different allergens. Welcoming substitute products into your operation without checking food labels is welcoming allergic reactions.

17. **Answer: B -** This is a problem because the new product contains allergens.

Checking food labels when receiving new product is important so that new allergens are not brought into your operation. If the ingredients in the substitute product change, chefs and cooks could prepare an allergen special order without realizing the offending allergen is in the dish.

18. **Answer: A -** A substituted product from a supplier that contains no additional allergens is an adequate substitution for a guest with allergies.

Checking labels on substituted products makes sure that new allergens are not being added to food. Even a small amount of an allergen could trigger an allergic reaction in an unsuspecting guest.

19. **Answer: B -** Food in storage is still at risk for cross-contact.

Proximity to a food containing allergens presents a risk of cross-contact for allergen-free foods. Foods that contain the Big 8 should be stored separately from foods used for allergen special orders.

20. **Answer: D -** Keeping allergen special order foods and regular foods together is not a good rule for food storage.

Keeping allergen special order foods separated from regular foods prevents cross-contact. Good storage rules to follow include keeping foods in sealed containers, clearly labeling foods, and keeping foods with allergens in separate containers.

Service

1. **Answer: B -** Cross-contact can be prevented by putting sauces on separate plates.

Allergen special orders should come into contact with as few other foods as possible to prevent their proteins being mixed. At pickup, the order should be confirmed as the allergen special order. Then no garnishes should be added, and sides and sauces should be served on separate plates.

2. **Answer: B -** There is still chance of cross-contact once the dish leaves the kitchen.

At pickup the server should confirm that it is indeed an allergen-free meal, but there is still an opportunity for cross-contact to occur before the meal is delivered. This can be reduced by not adding garnishes and putting sides and sauces on separate plates. Then the allergen dish should not touch anything before it is carried by hand to the guest.

3. **Answer: C -** Cross-contact can be prevented by completely cooking food.

Cross-contact and cross-contamination are frequently confused. While cross-contamination can be prevented by fully cooking food, cross-contact cannot be corrected by cooking food. Once cross-contact has occurred, the only option is to discard the food.

4. **Answer: A -** During an emergency, an employee could help by waiting outside to signal the ambulance.

In the case of an emergency the most important task is to call 911. After this first step, making sure that emergency personal can find the guest in crisis is extremely helpful. Employees can all help by remaining calm.

5. **Answer: D -** Jose made errors when he added garnishes to the order and carried it stacked with other plates.

At pickup, the first step should be to confirm that the dish is the correct allergen-free order. Then, it should be carried by hand to the guest free of garnish and with sides and sauces on separate plates

6. **Answer: A -** Carrying multiple plates would not prevent cross-contact when serving food.

Keeping the allergen special order free from cross-contact requires keeping the dish away from all other foods. This includes dressings, sauces, garnishes, other guests' dishes, or any accidental spills.

7. **Answer: D -** Ricky did not make a mistake when confirming the dish then carrying it directly to the guest.

Ricky's example is a great illustration of preventing cross-contact. After confirming that the dish was correct, he bypassed all opportunities for cross-contact by skipping garnishing and taking the dish directly to the guest.

8. **Answer: B** - Putting the dish on a red plate could help a server recognize the allergen special order.

Color-coded systems are excellent ways to keep allergen special orders separate. In an operation that plated all allergen orders on red plates, this would be an easy way for servers to visually identify them.

9. **Answer: C** - Confirming the allergen special order would be the last step.

Before a server takes the order to the guest, verbally confirming that it is the correct allergen special order is crucial. After this, the server would put any sauces on separate plates and carry the order by hand to the guest.

10. **Answer: C** - A "May Contain" statement discloses that there might be small amounts of a food allergen in the product.

Manufacturers are not legally obligated to include "May Contain" lists the way they are required to list Big 8 allergens. These lists can be written many ways for example, "May Contain," "Allergy Information," or "Processed at a facility that also processes__________."

11. **Answer: B** - Manufacturers are NOT legally required to list "may contain" statements

Legally manufacturers are required to list the Big 8 allergens in the name of the product, in parentheses in the ingredient list, or in a "contains list." Many manufacturers include may contain statements for ingredients that may be found in trace amounts.

12. **Answer: B** - Guests with food allergies may order off the menu or use a self-service station

Sometimes guests with food allergies stick to ordering off of the menu; however, this is not always the case and food allergy safety is important at a self-service station. One way to maintain safety is to place items with allergens away from other items at the station.

13. **Answer: B** - Making items easy to reach is a way to improve a self service station

Along with being well-stocked and clean, a station should be accessible. When items are easier to reach there is a lower chance of cross-contact because foods are less likely to mix.

14. **Answer: B** - Designating utensils for each item is a good rule for maintaining a self-service station

Cross-contact of food proteins can occur with shared utensils. Designating utensils for each self-service station item is one way to prevent cross-contact and provide a safe station.

15. **Answer: C -** Accurate signage and placing items with allergens away from those without allergens illustrate best practices for a self-service station.

There are four ways to best maintain safety at a self-service station for guests with food allergies. Providing informational signs and positioning items with allergens away from those without allergens are two examples. Not mixing old food with new food and designating utensils for each food are also examples.

16. **Answer: D -** By adding new food into an existing container, Jamie is mixing new food into old food.

It is important not to mix new product into old product. This increases the likelihood of cross-contact.

17. **Answer: B -** Using dedicated cleaning equipment is a way to prevent cross-contact.

Cleaning with spray bottles and paper towels work best to prevent cross-contact. By using spray bottles of cleanser, rinse, and sanitizer with disposable paper towels, cross-contact is prevented because food proteins are not spread around.

18. **Answer: B -** It is equally important to keep self-service and work stations cleaned.

These stations should be cleaned with the same methods and frequency. Both are areas where cross-contact could occur and must be cleaned thoroughly.

19. **Answer: B -** Using the same tongs for muffins and hard-boiled eggs is an example of cross-contact.

For this reason, having designated utensils for different items in the self-service area is important. Items in the self-service area can also be labeled with informational signs identifying wheat and eggs as allergens.

20. **Answer: A -** All packaged foods on a self service station need to be labeled for allergens.

Using packaged foods is one way to lower the risk of cross-contact. When these products are labeled correctly guests are unlikely to experience allergic reactions from them.

21. **Answer: C -** For refills, a server should replace the items instead of refilling them

Bread and drinks are both potential allergens. Replacing the product rather than refilling it reduces the risk of cross-contact.